COMMON COURTESY IS FREE
AN ETIQUETTE HANDBOOK

1ST EDITION

Tamlyn L. Franklin

Common Courtesy is Free ©2020 Tamlyn L. Franklin

ISBN: 978-1-7341797-8-1

All rights reserved. This book is protected under the copyright laws of the United States of America.

No portion of this book may be reproduced, distributed, or transmitted in any form, including photocopying, recording, or other electronic or mechanical methods, without the written permission of the publisher, except in the case of brief quotations embodied in reviews and certain other non-commercial uses permitted by copyright law. Permission granted on request.

Published by LaBoo Publishing Enterprise

For information regarding special discounts for bulk purchases, please contact the publisher:

LaBoo Publishing Enterprise, LLC
staff@laboopublishing.com
www.laboopublishing.com

Printed in the United States of America

Introduction

My two favorite sayings are: "Common courtesy is free," and "Common courtesy doesn't take much time and doesn't cost a dime." For the last few years, I've shared etiquette tips in workshops, in general conversations, with family, friends, and my followers on social media. Etiquette tips about dining, dealing with friends, business matters, holidays, and seasonal changes, are included in this helpful guide. I've gathered etiquette (also known as *manners*) over the years just from living and learning firsthand from mentors, parents, grandparents, teachers, children, spouses, siblings, enemies, and friends.

Social rules are constantly changing because we're moving at a rapid-fire pace, but some things will never change when it comes to having good manners. I hope my words of wisdom that are sprinkled throughout will motivate you and inspire you to have common courtesy for others.

Who should read this book? If you're young, mature, seasoned, just starting out in your career, or just want to be in the know about common courtesy, then this book is for you.

There's more to come: I couldn't fill all my etiquette wisdom in this small handbook, so more will be coming later in another edition. Stay tuned.

Tamlyn L. Franklin

Other books by Tamlyn Franklin

Essentials of Dining Etiquette:
A guide to understanding and
mastering dining rules

How to Become an Unstoppable Black Woman

Other books
by Jacalyn Franklin

Acknowledgements

My grateful thanks to my family, friends, social media followers, teachers, editors, graphic artists and all those who have nurtured and helped with this project

To Amani, Amari, Braxton, Chnye,
Riley, Ziay, and Zuri

Airplane Etiquette: When de-boarding the plane, wait your turn, exit row by row. Don't jump your fellow passengers to be the first one off the plane.

• • • • • • •

Airplane Etiquette: Keep your shoes on if you have a foot odor problem. Others will surely notice.

• • • • • • •

Airplane Etiquette: Don't hog the armrests.

• • • • • • •

Airplane Etiquette: If you spill a drink on someone or on their belongings, immediately apologize and offer to pay for damages or dry cleaning.

• • • • • • •

Airplane Etiquette: Avoid lingering in aisles. Be considerate of flight attendants—especially when food and beverage carts are in use—and your fellow passengers.

• • • • • • •

Airplane Etiquette: Use your armrest to pull yourself up. Don't use the back of the seat in front of you as leverage when getting up.

• • • • • • •

Airplane Etiquette: Never force a conversation on your neighbor. Enough said.

• • • • • • •

Airplane Etiquette: Don't recline your seat all the way. Consider the person behind you.

• • • • • • •

Airplane Etiquette: Avoid irritating your neighbors and keep the sound level down on your earphones. Use the arm-length rule: If you hold out your earphone at arms-length and can hear the sound, so can everyone else. Simply turn it down.

• • • • • • •

Airplane Etiquette: Sit in your assigned seat until everyone has boarded. You can switch seats after the doors have been closed and empty seats have been determined.

• • • • • • •

Airplane Etiquette: Wait for colleagues at the gate. Don't clog up the jet-way. This will allow everyone to exit quickly.

• • • • • • •

Attitude Etiquette Tip: Go to work or place of business dressed your best and have a positive, can-do attitude. Avoid dressing and acting like Friday can't come soon enough. Also, dress as if you're interviewing for a higher position because people who have the power to promote or demote you are watching you. Good habits will yield great results, both personally and professionally.

•••••••

Attitude: "Your best asset is your attitude."

•••••••

Autumn Etiquette Tip: Check the weather before getting dressed. Autumn weather is unpredictable. One day could be sunny and 85 degrees, and the next day could bring snow. It's a great time of year for sweaters, stylish socks, tights, ties, scarves, gloves, turtlenecks, etc. Have fun with accessories (men and women). Dress for the weather and let your style shine!

•••••••

Autumn Etiquette Tip: Dress appropriately raking leaves. Wear long sleeves, tuck pant legs into socks, and wear garden gloves to prevent contact with poison ivy and other plant life. Use insect repellent to help ward off mosquitoes and other insects (ticks).

> Success is a journey, not a destination.
>
> Ben Sweetland

•••••••

Autumn Etiquette Tip: If you use a gas-powered leaf blower, no matter the size, consider your neighbors and the noise level. Refrain from using a leaf blower before 9 a.m., especially on the weekend. Nothing is more annoying, especially after a long work week, than to wake, before the crack of dawn to the sound of loud lawn equipment.

•••••••

Autumn Etiquette Tip: Don't blow leaves from your property to your neighbor's property, even if your neighbor's trees are causing you grief. Remember, leaves that fall on your property are your responsibility.

•••••••

Autumn Etiquette Tip: Don't pile leaves on your property and leave them for several days with the hope they will not blow away. After you rake the leaves, bag them immediately and store them for recycling or place them for pickup.

•••••••

Autumn Etiquette Tip: As trees begin to shed their leaves, homeowners (with trees) should prepare for the deluge of leaves. Remember, if leaves fall on your property, no matter who owns the tree (you or your neighbor), each homeowner is responsible for raking their own property.

●●●●●●●

Business Etiquette Wardrobe Trivia: After work, my friend and I are going directly to dinner. Can I wear a fancy blouse to work (can he wear a fancy necktie to work)? Answer: After-hour activities should not dictate work attire. Take along a blouse or shirt and suitable tie for the evening to work. After work, change into your evening outfit. Women should be mindful of garments that reveal more than is appropriate in a business setting.

●●●●●●●

Business Meal Tip: Before you plan a business meal, do your homework. Find out if your client(s) have any dietary restrictions. Some people may not eat meat on Fridays in observing religious traditions, and some people may not eat pork, seafood, etc. It's

> "Common" courtesy doesn't cost a dime and doesn't take much time.
>
> Tamlyn Franklin

a best practice to find to discreetly learn about eating restrictions and/or preferences beforehand.

• • • • • • •

Business Meeting Tip: Be on time. If you are going to be late, please call in advance and apologize. Lateness can be seen as disrespectful and inefficient.

• • • • • • •

Business Tip: *Avoid lethal phrases:*
   "There's nothing I can do."
   "It's our policy."
   "It's not my job."
   "Please call/come back."
   "I can't…."

• • • • • • •

Business Tip: Use Uplifting Phrases:
"Thank you…"
"I would be happy to…"
"It's my pleasure…"
"Is there anything else I can do?"
"You're welcome."

• • • • • • •

Cancer Etiquette: Stay connected. Don't disappear when someone close to you is diagnosed. This is the time to call, visit, and check in with them. Your friend/loved one needs to know that you care and haven't written him or her off.

• • • • • • •

Cancer Etiquette: Don't touch or pull on a cancer victim's hair (person who may be undergoing or recently completed chemotherapy treatment). Don't ask someone with cancer how it feels to be bald. Avoid saying, "It's only hair."

• • • • • • •

Cancer Etiquette: If a friend or family member shares his/her shocking cancer diagnosis with you, keep your composure and offer sincere prayers and comforting words, example, say, "I'm so sorry." Avoid crying hysterically or asking, "Why? Why did this have to happen to you?" Remember, it took courage for the person to share the news, so the diagnosis isn't about you.

• • • • • • •

Cancer Etiquette: If someone you know has lost a loved one to cancer, don't ever ask the person if he or she is over the person's death. There is no set amount of time for a person to grieve. These questions are extremely insensitive and highly offensive.

• • • • • • •

Cancer Etiquette: If it's revealed to you that someone you know has cancer, refrain from contacting the person with the diagnosis. Don't assume the person's illness is terminal. Respect the person's privacy.

• • • • • • •

Cancer Etiquette: If you encounter someone who may be in remission, don't bring up the illness (cancer) each time you see him or her. Just say, "It's great seeing you" and talk about something else (current events, etc.).

• • • • • • •

Cancer Etiquette: Offer kind words to someone suffering with cancer, such as "I hope everything will be all right." "You will be in excellent care." or "You're in an excellent program." If you're at a loss for words, say, "I'm really sorry." "I love you." or "My prayers are with you."

• • • • • • •

> Children will not remember you for the material things you provided, but for the feeling that you cherished them.
>
> Richard L. Evans

Cancer Etiquette: Don't underestimate the power of your presence. A hug, a gentle touch, a listening ear, or even a small gift can be comforting. Small gift ideas: books, DVDs, movie tickets, or healthy snacks.

•••••••

Cancer Etiquette: Avoid commenting on the appearance of someone who has cancer. Never tell someone how badly they look (skinny, dry, sickly, ashy, gray, bald). You have no idea how hurtful your comments may be. Instead say, "You're looking stronger." or "I'm glad to see you're walking around."

•••••••

Cancer Etiquette: Offer to lend a hand and be specific about what you can do to help. Offer to drive the person dealing with cancer to a doctor's appointment, cook a meal, provide his or her favorite dish, rake the leaves, or babysit. What may seem like a small gesture to you may be greatly appreciated by the person struggling with the illness.

• • • • • • •

Cancer Etiquette: Don't ask "Are you cancer free now?" There is no such thing as cancer free.

• • • • • • •

Cancer Etiquette: Don't look up the odds or other statistics. Don't point out the odds or suggest alternative treatments or breakthroughs. Your findings may confirm the cancer victim's worst nightmare, or your suggestions may put the cancer patient (or his/her family) in a terrible predicament. Just remember, people want to focus on living.

Cancer Etiquette: If someone with cancer wants to talk, let him or her set the tone for the conversation. Don't overtake the conversation. Spend more time listening than talking.

•••••••

Cancer Etiquette: Common courtesy should be extended to a friend, coworker, loved one or family member who may be struggling with cancer. The two most important things to remember: 1) Treat others the way you want to be treated; and 2) Think before you speak.

•••••••

Casual Friday Etiquette Tip: Casual Friday means something different for every company. Whatever your corporate policy is, avoid messy, dirty, ripped, or otherwise inappropriate outfits. One poor casual Friday outfit could prevent a future promotion.

•••••••

Cell Phone Etiquette Tip. Remember to silence your cell phone and disable alarms before attending meetings, worship services—a ringing cell phone is annoying to attendees and presenters. Either leave your cell phone in a safe place or turn it off when entering a building, meeting, or event.

•••••••

Cell Phone Etiquette Tip: Avoid emotional conversations in public.

•••••••

Cell Phone Etiquette Tip: Don't text during a meeting or conference. Give the speaker your undivided attention. Imagine if you are the speaker.

•••••••

Cell Phone Etiquette Tip: Do not put your phone on speaker without notifying the person on the other end.

•••••••

Cell Phone Etiquette Tip: Never send a text message with sexual overtones or one that could appear as a threat.

•••••••

Cell Phone Etiquette Tip: Avoid taking personal calls during business meetings. This includes interviews and meetings with coworkers or subordinates.

•••••••

Cell Phone Etiquette Tip: Parents, establish phone-free times or zones for your children's phones. This can free them from the temptation of wondering if a text message has arrived, etc.

•••••••

Cell Phone Etiquette Tip (in theaters). Turn your phone off before you enter the theater. If you are anticipating a call (from a parent, spouse, friend, child or sitter, etc.), place your phone on vibrate. If your phone rings, don't answer it in the theater. Step out into the lobby to call the person back. Don't light up your phone's screen in a darkened theater to check the time, text, or talk. Be considerate to others.

•••••••

Cell Phone Etiquette Tip: Avoid personal topics when others can hear you.

•••••••

Cell Phone Etiquette Tip: Avoid texting and driving. Talking and texting while driving are prohibited in some states.

> Common courtesy is free. TLF
>
> You should never be too busy to say "hello," "please," and "thank you."

●●●●●●●

Cell Phone Etiquette Tip: Avoid inappropriate profile pictures. Many high-quality cell phones show your picture on the screen when you call.

●●●●●●●

Cell Phone Etiquette Tip: Avoid taking calls when you're already engaged in a face-to-face conversation with someone or a group of people. If you must take the call, ask permission. Remember, we should treat everyone with common decency and respect.

●●●●●●●

Cell Phone Etiquette Tip: Put your phone's ringer on silent mode in medical facilities, worship or religious service, theaters, and restaurants.

∙∙∙∙∙∙∙

Cell Phone Etiquette Tip: Lower your voice when taking calls in public. Consider the people around you–they will hear your conversation.

∙∙∙∙∙∙∙

Cell Phone Etiquette Tip: Don't put your phone on speaker. People do not want to hear your conversation, nor do they want to hear the person on the other end.

∙∙∙∙∙∙∙

CHANGE: If we change the way we look at things, then the things we look at will change.

∙∙∙∙∙∙∙

Choose civility (politeness) over incivility (deliberate discourtesy).

> All transactions and relationships are enriched by courtesy.
>
> Unknown

•••••••

How to Dress: Wear clothes that are seasonally appropriate. Use common sense. Avoid wooly turtlenecks in summer and avoid wearing linen during the winter. If you are unsure about the dress code for a specific event, ask the host.

•••••••

Coffee Shop Etiquette: If you're in the middle of a phone conversation walking into a coffee shop, kindly ask the person on the other end if you can place him or her on hold or call back later after you place your order. Also, when you're placing your order, hold off texting, sending or checking email, checking voicemail, or making a call.

•••••••

Coffee Shop Etiquette Tip: Share the outlets. Consider others when you plug multiple devices into outlets. Leave an outlet for someone else, especially if your battery is fully charged.

● ● ● ● ● ● ●

College Roommate Etiquette Tip: Always ask permission to use your roommate's belongings. Don't assume you can borrow his or her laptop or other items.

● ● ● ● ● ● ●

College Roommate Etiquette Tip: Be considerate. If your roommate asks for quiet time to complete a project or assignment, you should oblige and make arrangements. Chances are that you will have to make a similar request at some point during the school year. Treat your roommate (others) the way you want to be treated.

● ● ● ● ● ● ●

College Roommate Etiquette Tip: Don't snoop. Although it may be tempting to snoop, avoid doing this. Consider how you would feel if you caught your roommate snooping through your things. Always ask permission to use your roommate's belongings. Don't assume that you can borrow their laptop or other items. In the same vein, always ask permission to invite friends over. You wouldn't want to have your roommate's friend or friends crash in your room without your permission.

•••••••

College Roommate Etiquette Tip: Share your concerns. Everyone has annoying habits. If your roommate has a habit or a behavior that annoys you, voice your frustration with your roommate and not to anyone who will listen. Discuss your concerns with your roommate and try to resolve the situation amicably.

•••••••

College Roommate Etiquette Tip: Clean up after yourself. Yes, sharing living space with someone else can be challenging. Do your best to keep common areas clean: pick up trash, clothes, books, and other items. Consider your roommate. Remember, it's not just your room. Your roommate will appreciate your cleanliness and thoughtfulness.

•••••••

Cookout / Barbecue Etiquette Tip: If you offer to make a side dish or bring a dessert, don't back out at the last minute, the host is counting on you. On the flip side, if the host says not to bring anything, don't. But always ask, just in case.

•••••••

Cookout/ Barbecue Etiquette Tip: If there is a food item you find exceptionally tasty, consider that other guests may enjoy the same item. For example, if the ribs are tender and flavorful, don't pile your plate with a full rack or half of a slab. Instead, take one piece of rib to complement the other delicious items you put on your plate.

●●●●●●●

Cookout / Barbecue Etiquette Tip: Cookouts and barbecues are a part of summer fun! Keep it stress-free for the host, hostess, and other guests and be considerate (common courtesy). Always RSVP to an invitation. See RSVP for other references.

●●●●●●●

Cyber Etiquette Tip: Social networking is a huge part of our culture. As communication on the Internet increases, so does the use of acronyms. Most people know that LOL means *laughing out loud*. Here are few other cyber acronyms to commit to memory:

TTYL – Talk to you later

SFW – Safe for work

FWIW – For what it's worth

AYOR – At your own risk
B4N – Bye for now
EML – Email me later
JK – Just kidding
B/C – Because
ROTFL – Rolling on the floor laughing
DF – Dear friend

•••••••

Cyber Etiquette Reminder: Everything you post online is public. It doesn't matter whether or not you delete the email or text message. If you publish something, it's traceable. This is your "cyber fingerprint".

•••••••

Dining Etiquette Tip: Beverages. It is considered good manners to wait until you have finished chewing and swallowed your food before sipping your beverage.

• • • • • • •

Dining Etiquette Tip: Dining with a prospective employer? Consider a meal with a potential employer as part of the interview process. Enter the chair from the left and exit from the right.

• • • • • • •

Dining Etiquette Tip: Dining with employees? Keep the conversation light. Find common topics of interest that are not controversial (i.e., sports, travel).

• • • • • • •

Dining Etiquette Tip: Dining with employees or coworkers? Do not neglect anyone sitting near you.

• • • • • • •

Dining Etiquette Ordering Tip: Demitasse: \⸱de-mi-⸱tas\ – small coffee cup.

Dining Etiquette Ordering Tip: Café au lait: \ka-ˌfˉa-ˉo-'lˉa\ – coffee with hot milk.

•••••••

Dining Etiquette Tip: After you finish eating your meal, do not push your plate away from you, start to clean the table, or begin to stack dishes. Wait until dishes are removed by the wait staff. This shows that you are well-mannered.

•••••••

Dining Etiquette Tip: If food gets stuck in your teeth while at the table, do not pick your teeth (with fingers or other objects such as matches and business cards), floss your teeth, use a tooth pick, or pull out a mirror to check your teeth at the table. Excuse yourself from the table and go to the bathroom to clean your teeth.

> **The Etiquette Consulting Group –**
> **The E stands for Excellence.**
> **The C stands for Civility.**
> **The G stands for Graciousness.**
>
> theetiquetteconsultinggroup.com

•••••••

Dining Etiquette Tip: Chew with a closed mouth.

•••••••

Driving Trivia: Did you know the only thing that can help someone sober up is the amount of time that passes after the last drink. Drinking strong coffee, exercising, or taking a cold shower will not.

•••••••

Driving Fact: Every two minutes a person is injured in a drunk-driving crash.

•••••••

Driving Etiquette Friendly Reminder: Treat others (fellow drivers, pedestrians, and bikers) the way you want to be treated. Conforming to the rules of the road and common courtesy helps to maintain order and avoid crashes. Here are tips to reduce the possibility of becoming involved in an aggressive driving incident:

- Allow extra time to travel
- Be patient
- Be courteous
- Concentrate on your driving behavior
- Always signal your intentions
- Obey all traffic laws, signs, signals and pavement markings
- Yield the right of way
- Avoid competing with other drivers.
- Get to your destination alive.

•••••••

Driving Etiquette Tip: Keep your eyes on the road. Resist the urge to text while driving. This is a challenge for experienced drivers because we think we know what we are doing. If you're like me, you think of everything you need to do and who you need to call or text while driving. In most states, it is against the law to text and drive, but people do it anyway. Please pull off the road if you must text. Resist the urge to text while driving.

• • • • • • •

Driving Etiquette Tip: The left lane is for faster moving traffic and passing vehicles. If you drive at or below the speed limit in the passing lane and you notice another car or a long line of cars in your rear-view mirror, kindly move to the right and allow them to pass. Don't hold up the left lane or impede the flow of traffic because this can create road rage, unnecessary tailgating, and accidents. Be polite and move to the right.

• • • • • • •

Driving Trivia: Did you know that 11 teens die every day as a result of texting while driving?

∙ ∙ ∙ ∙ ∙ ∙ ∙

Email Etiquette Tip: When you send an email message, allow 48 hours for a response. Do not assume that your message has been received and/or read. If it's an urgent matter, call.

∙ ∙ ∙ ∙ ∙ ∙ ∙

Email Etiquette Tip: Always include a brief message that accurately reflects the content of your email in the Subject field. Neglecting to do so can cause your email to be flagged as spam. Sometimes, in haste, this can easily be forgotten.

∙ ∙ ∙ ∙ ∙ ∙ ∙

Email Etiquette Tip: Ensure that your (work-related) email includes a courteous greeting (example, Hello, John,) and closing (example, Regards, Best regards, Sincerely, etc.). Doing so helps to make your email seem courteous and not seem demanding or rude.

• • • • • • •

Email Etiquette Tip: When you receive a work-related email, respond within one business day. Sometimes, we don't know the complete answer or we don't have time to respond. When this is the case, acknowledge that the email has been received, provide a time when you will have the complete answer, or direct or guide the sender to someone you know who can address the need. The bottom line, as a common courtesy, is to respond.

• • • • • • •

Email Etiquette Tip: Do not type in all caps. Sending an email message with all capital letters is perceived as screaming or yelling your message. Also, various studies have indicated that it is more difficult and takes longer to read text that is typed in all caps. To avoid misinterpretation and to convey a clear message, use upper and lowercase letters. I love the quote by Dale Carnegie, "There are four ways, and only four ways, in which we have contact with the world. We are evaluated and classified by these four contacts: what we do, how we look, what we say, and how we say it."

• • • • • • •

Email Etiquette Tip: Keep email messages brief as most of us receive far too many. Consider only cc'ing people who really need to know. It is overwhelming to filter through a barrage of messages that do not require action or attention.

• • • • • • •

Email Etiquette Tip: Be mindful what you share via email and voicemail with coworkers. Oftentimes, people may use information you share with them against you. Rule of thumb: Share only what you don't mind everyone seeing, hearing, or knowing.

• • • • • • •

> We are what we repeatedly do. Excellence, therefore, is not an act but a habit.
>
> Aristotle

Etiquette is about being comfortable in any situation and making others feel comfortable around you. Sometimes we fall short. It's alright. Keep trying. Be better today than you were yesterday. Mistakes are proof that you are trying.

• • • • • • •

Etiquette is not being stuffy. It's just a fancy word for being comfortable and making others feel comfortable around you in every situation. Etiquette tips are gentle reminders to be courteous and considerate in every situation (home, school, interview, workplace, church, library, dorm, public places, parties, reunions, galas, etc.)! *Common courtesy is free. TLF*

• • • • • • •

Today is a new day. We each have the **power to choose.** We can choose cowardly or courageous; we can play it safe or take a stand; we can draw back or go boldly; we can let fear consume us or we can exercise faith; we can be discouraged and despondent or we can be optimistic and hopeful. We have the power to choose. What do you choose? Choose polite over rude.

• • • • • • •

Ex-Etiquette Tip: The best advice when dealing with an ex is put the children first. Do what is in the best interest of the children. Children need love and a safe environment. Whenever either adult is not sure of what to do, both should ask one simple question: Do you really think that is in his/her (child's) best interest?"

• • • • • • •

Ex-Etiquette Tip: Exes who have children together should try to be civil with each other, especially around the children, no matter how difficult it may be. Both parents should be thoughtful of and accountable to their children. Neither parent should neglect their children or withhold their love and/or support from their children. Children do not deserve anything except unconditional love and support.

•••••••

Facebook Etiquette Tip: When someone posts something on FB, avoid adding unrelated comments to the post; this can be very offensive. Start a new thread if you have a comment on a different subject. Or, send a private message or inbox the person.

•••••••

Facebook Etiquette Tip: Ignoring is acceptable. You are under no obligation to acknowledge a Facebook friend request, whether it comes from a friend or a stranger. This is equivalent to allowing visitors to sit at your dinner table if they showed up without an invitation at your house at 6 p.m. You wouldn't feel obliged to let them in.

●●●●●●●

Facebook Etiquette Tip: Don't be overly sensitive… If a Facebook friend or relative neglects to comment on your status or congratulate you on something you are celebrating (graduation, birthday, or birth of a child), don't allow their lack of attention to your status to ruin an otherwise good relationship. Don't take it personal; chalk it up to forgetfulness.

●●●●●●●

Facebook Etiquette Tip: Use Facebook chat sparingly. Just because someone has a Facebook window open doesn't mean they're available for a chat session, especially during business hours. Don't be offended if you do not get an instant response. Recognize that your friends may be too busy to respond immediately.

•••••••

Fitness Center Etiquette: Avoid making too much noise; talking too much, excessive grunting, cell phone ringing, yelling, and cursing. Other exercisers are trying to concentrate on their workouts too. Loud and constant noises can irritate other exercisers. I desperately wanted to post this tip at the gym one morning when the person running on the treadmill grunted very loudly the entire time she ran...Annoying!!! She received disturbing looks from all exercisers on the cardio machines, including me.

•••••••

Fitness Center Etiquette: Turn your headphones down. Some folks have their volume up so loud they might as well not wear headphones. As a general rule, if you hold out your earphone at arms-length and can hear it, so can everyone else. Simply turn it down.

•••••••

Fitness Center Etiquette: If you are sick (coughing, sneezing, etc.), then take a day off from the gym. Other gym members will appreciate your thoughtfulness.

> The golden rule for every businessman: "Put yourself in your customer's place."
>
> Orison Swett Marden

• • • • • • •

Fitness Center Etiquette: When exercising in a public place such as a fitness center, health club, or outdoor track/field, be mindful of the written and unwritten rules of etiquette. Avoid loud cell phone conversations. Loud and constant noises can annoy other exercisers.

• • • • • • •

Friendly Reminder: Forgive like you want to be forgiven.

•••••••

Friendship Reminder: Don't allow online interactions to ruin or breakup real-life relationships. Online interactions can lead to a lot of miscommunication and hurt. If something is said directly to or about you on Facebook that is hurtful or of concern to you, from a close friend or loved one, aim to resolve issues as you would for other "offline" issues.

•••••••

Gift Giving Etiquette (at the office) Tip: Avoid giving personal gifts: flowers, candy, jewelry or other items that could send a far more romantic message between an employer and employee and between co-workers. Instead, choose professional gifts such as a pen set, a paperweight, or other office supplies. Gifts.com (http://www.gifts.com/office-gifts.html) has great office and coworker gift ideas for Christmas, birthdays and more!

Gift Giving Etiquette (at the Office): Gift giving is a natural part of the holidays. When it comes to giving gifts to colleagues or your boss, keep in mind that there may be written company policies concerning gift exchanges. For obvious reasons, some companies have a "no-gift" policy. If there is a policy at your company, be sure to follow the "rules" for how much you spend and what type of gift you buy. In the United States, $50 is considered a nominal value. Whether there is a written policy or not, be extra sensitive about the gift you choose, the impact it can have on other people, or the effect that it can have on your professional reputation.

The Golden Rule – Consider the Golden Rule in all your activities (personal and professional) …Treat others the way you want to be treated or do unto others as you would have them do unto you.

> Kindness is the language which the deaf can hear and blind can see.
>
> Mark Twain

•••••••

Exercise the Golden Rule – Do unto others as you would have them do unto you. If you wouldn't speak to the person that way face to face then don't do it online. Remember the adage, "If you can't say anything nice, then say nothing at all."

•••••••

Gentle Reminder: "The first stage or indicator of grief is denial. We must be willing to acknowledge that we are grieving what or whoever we have lost so that we can begin to heal...we can't effectively heal from a splinter unless we are willing to acknowledge it's there, experience the pain from removing it, and allowing time to heal afterwards." Alicia Dorn

•••••••

Gentle Reminder: Most people feel obligated to say something when someone is hurting. It's okay not to know what to say. Nonverbal communication (i.e., a hug) says a lot and can be a direct source of comfort. Never underestimate something as simple as your presence (just being there).

●●●●●●●

Gentle Reminder: Offer kind words to someone who is grieving. If you don't know what to say, it's OK. Say, "I'm really sorry." "I love you." or "My prayers are with you."

●●●●●●●

Gentle Reminder: Dealing with grief is a lonely business. At anytime someone can be grieving. The loss could be a divorce, a separation, an empty nest, loss of employment or a friendship, or death of a pet or loved one. If someone you know is grieving, you should always honor any/all requests of the person who has suffered a loss. Example, please do not send flowers or donations in lieu of flowers. And if you ask what the grieving person needs, follow his or her request. If the person wants to be alone for a while, grant that request. Your compliance will be appreciated.

•••••••

Gentle Reminder: If a friend has suffered a loss, he/she will continue to need your support for many months to come. Don't disappear and don't exclude your friend from activities you think he or she is not ready to join. Send a card, encouraging note, or make a phone call on a regular basis. Continue to include your friend on your social plans; he or she will let you know when to the time is right to participate. Ask your friend to lunch, dinner or other outings.

•••••••

Gentle Reminder: If you are speaking to someone who is grieving, do not launch into your own grief story. Be a good listener and put the other person first. While your story may be helpful, it may not be helpful at the time. Remember, this is about your friend's needs and story, not yours.

•••••••

Gentle Reminder: When someone loses a loved one, there is no time limit on grieving. It is extremely insensitive to suggest to someone when they should be over a loss. For example, if someone suffered the loss of a loved one, one week, one month, one year, or one decade ago, you should never ever say to them, "aren't you over it yet". Your comments can cut very deep. Don't make comments that would diminish the importance of the loss. Comments such as "I've been through this myself," "she/he was suffering so much, death was a blessing," or "you are young, you will marry again," are not comforting to the bereaved. Grieving takes time!

•••••••

Gentle Reminder: Do not feel uncomfortable if you or the bereaved becomes emotional or begins to cry. Grieving is a natural part of the healing process. If you or the bereaved become extremely upset, it would be best to excuse yourself to minimize the strain on the family.

• • • • • • •

Gentlemen: Some common courtesies have been forgotten or never been taught to some men (young and mature). However, there are plenty of gentlemen (well-bred men) out there, and chivalry is alive!

• • • • • • •

Ladies / Women: The way we speak, dress, and look communicate to people around us. It tells how much we respect ourselves, our bodies, and what type of person we are. Some common tips have been forgotten or never been taught to some women (young and mature). However, there are many ladies (well-bred women) who know what is proper for women.

•••••••

Ladies / Women should maintain carefully pedicured feet. Fingernails and toenails should be clean and shaped. The length of the nail is a matter of lifestyle preference. If a woman chooses to wear polish, it should not be chipped.

•••••••

Ladies / Women should ensure that her legs and underarms are meticulously groomed.

•••••••

Ladies / Women Wardrobe: Clothes should be clean, neat, and wrinkle free. Perfume should be minimal. Women should make every effort to avoid too much: makeup, jewelry; or attire that is too casual (for certain occasions): too low cut, too tight, etc.

•••••••

Self-invited Guest Etiquette Tip: If you have self-invited guests and you wish for them to leave, you can say, "I'd invite you to stay, but I'm busy at the moment." or "I have a deadline to meet. Maybe you can stop by some other time."

•••••••

Uninvited Guest Etiquette: Don't take uninvited guests to your friends' home, barbeque, or party without giving the host advance notice. This gives the host time to consider the extra guest. Don't be offended if the host does not oblige. At small barbeques and dinner parties, the host may be able and willing to accommodate a few extra guests, but there are no guarantees. At large events such as weddings and receptions, there is usually a per-plate fee, so extra guests can cause unnecessary stress for the host. Sometimes, the host will not indicate an "adults only" event. The invitation envelope has the name of the person/persons who are invited. For example: Mr. & Mrs. John Jones; Ms. Tia Jackson; Mr. James Adams; Mr. & Mrs. Jones and family. Only take those who were invited.

If you have been invited to a party and really want to go, but have house guests of your own, give the hostess a chance to invite you some other time. Say something like, "Mary, I would love to attend, but my two nieces and nephew will be with me that day, and I'm not sure if it would be a good idea to bring them."

> You gain strength, experience and confidence by every experience where you really stop to look fear in the face. You must do the thing you cannot do.
>
> Eleanor Roosevelt

• • • • • • •

Gym Etiquette Tip: Music can motivate you and make your workout fun. But if headphones are played loudly, music can become a distraction to other gym goers. A good rule of thumb is to take your

> **Physical strength is measured by what we can carry; spiritual by what we can bear.**
>
> Author Unknown

headphones off and hold them at an arm's length. Keep the volume at your preferred level. If you can still hear your music, clearly or otherwise, it's too loud. If you're sitting next to someone and they can hear your music, it's also too loud. Consider others as they workout. Enjoy your workout and your music.

• • • • • • •

Gym Etiquette Tip: Keep your sweat to yourself. Carry a towel to wipe off a bench or machine you use. Nothing is more disturbing as picking up a slippery weight or lying down in a stranger's pool of sweat. If you forget to bring a towel, use paper towels at the gym. Consider others.

•••••••

Halloween Etiquette Tip: If you have leftover candy from Halloween, don't fret. Donate leftovers to a local school or church or give your coworkers a sweet treat.

•••••••

Halloween Etiquette Tip: Drive with extra care. At dusk on Halloween, streets and sidewalks may be peppered with children, some not chaperoned by a responsible adult. Take extra care when driving in residential areas. Honor all stop signs and avoid speeding.

•••••••

Halloween Etiquette Tip: Turn off your porch and outdoor lights. If you do not plan to hand out candy, run out of candy sooner than you thought, or no longer want to answer the door, turn off your lights. This is a universal signal for Trick or Treaters to bypass your house.

•••••••

Halloween Etiquette Tip: Don't spoil the fun. Halloween is the one time of year when kids expect to receive candy. Don't ruin the fun by handing out crayons, coloring books, tooth brushes, dental floss, and other inedible items that you think are useful. Let children enjoy endless sugar *for one night*. Also, don't hand out homemade goodies (cookies, candy apples, brownies, etc.) unless you know the Trick or Treaters quite well. Most parents will not allow their children to eat homemade goods from strangers.

•••••••

Halloween Etiquette Tip: Dress Appropriately. Halloween parties and costume contests will be enjoyed in schools and on many jobs. Whether you're 3 or 63, inappropriate costumes are distasteful. Keep it classy and age appropriate. For example, dressing as a stripper may be a good idea to you, but could be very offensive to your boss and/or coworkers. Be thoughtful about your costume. Aim to have a good time and maintain your professionalism.

When you have the opportunity to be brilliant or pleasant, choose pleasant.

•••••••

Happy Hour Etiquette Tip: If you plan to drink alcohol, do not take a chance and drive. Designate a driver or plan for a car service.

•••••••

Holiday Etiquette Tip: Try not worry if you don't have material things to give or you don't have anyone to give gifts to. Free gifts are at your disposal. Here are three priceless and life- changing gifts.

1. Time – Spend quality time with the person or people in your life who cherish your presence. Or spend quality time alone—reflecting on where

and how far you have come and the endless possibilities of where your journey will take you.

2. Forgiveness – Forgive yourself for mistakes you have made or people you have hurt and anything else that may be hindering you. Forgive others for hurting you, leaving or abandoning you, mistreating or abusing you, not loving you, not coming to your rescue, not helping you in or through a storm or anything else that may be hindering your relationship(s) or your progress.

3. Love – Give love. Love unconditionally. Love never fails. It's the reason for the season. Happy Holidays!!!!!

•••••••

Holiday Etiquette: Invitations – The moment you receive an invitation or RSVP, reply in the manner indicated on the invitation (e.g., phone call or email) within a few days. RSVP is French and means

"Répondez s'il vous plait; meaning "Reply please" or "Please respond." Neglecting to promptly reply with your intention can cause the host grief preparing for the event.

• • • • • • •

Holiday Etiquette: Thank-you notes are ways to express gratitude for acts of kindness and generosity. The note should be sent within a few days and no more than a few weeks of receiving the gift. Hand write thank-you notes to express your thoughts about the gift on the day you receive the gift. Email messages and instant messages are no substitute for this small but meaningful gesture.

• • • • • • •

Holiday Etiquette: Care should be taken when attending any holiday shindig, especially the office party. Avoid overdoing anything (dressing inappropriately, drinking too much, dancing too provocatively, flirting with coworkers, etc.). Everything should be done in moderation. Aim to have a good time but maintain your professionalism. Remember, when the party ends, you will have to face your coworkers or boss again. Holidays are typically the time for giving gifts, spending time with family and friends, and enjoying special moments. Use these tips to help you get through the holidays with style and grace.

• • • • • • •

Holiday Etiquette: During the busy holiday season, let's be mindful of travel etiquette, especially on airplanes, where space is limited. (see Airplane Etiquette)

• • • • • • •

Holiday Invitation Etiquette Tip:

Thanksgiving marks the beginning of the holiday season. As you start to receive invitations to holiday celebrations, dinner parties, office parties, galas, and any other celebratory affairs, *remember to respond to the invitation.* The moment you receive an invitation, RSVP or reply in the manner indicated on the invitation (e.g., response card, telephone call, or email) within a few days. Replying to the invitation or sending your RSVP is the simple code that tells your host whether you are attending. This helps the host tremendously. Neglecting to promptly reply with your intention can cause the host grief (time, energy and money) when preparing for the event.

> The important thing is not being afraid to take a chance. Remember, the greatest failure is to not try. Once you find something you love to do, be the best at doing it.
>
> Debbi Fields

• • • • • • •

> "Integrity has no need for rules."

Holiday Party Etiquette Tip: Always RSVP.

•••••••

Holiday Party Eating Reminders/Tips: As the New Year approaches and holiday parties continue, be ready to greet and be greeted by others. Maintain clean hands:

- Do not walk around with multiple hors D' oeuvres. Keep one hand free for greeting others
- Do not double dip your food
- Do not return buffet food
- Properly discard trash (napkins, toothpicks, dessert papers, etc.)

•••••••

Interview Etiquette Tip: Be prepared with a fresh copy of your well-written, spell-checked résumé; a copy of your diploma or other credentials (if required); and knowledge of a few facts about the company/

organization where you would like to work. This will require an investment of time and a bit of research on your part, but will pay huge dividends later.

•••••••

Interview Etiquette Tip: Do your homework. School may be over, but homework isn't. When you are fortunate to have been granted an interview with an employer, make it your business to arrive prepared for the interview by doing your homework. Homework means doing research about the company.

•••••••

Interview Etiquette Tip: Stay focused. Keep your cell phone and other electronic devices out of sight during the interview so you're not distracted. Do not send text messages or check your cell phone for messages during a job interview. Give you undivided attention to the interviewer. Checking messages during an interview is unacceptable.

> He who has a "why" to live can bear almost any how.
>
> **Friedrich Nietzsche**

•••••••

Interview Etiquette Tip: Be polite. The moment you enter a company/facility/organization, treat everyone you meet with kindness. Make eye contact, give sincere smiles and firm handshakes to each person you encounter at the company—from the receptionist to the president.

•••••••

Interview Etiquette Tip: If you happen to be at dinner while on an interview, never have more than one alcoholic beverage. If there is a bottle of wine on the table, and the waiter offers you another glass, simply place a hand over the top of your glass. This is a polite way of signifying "no to more wine."

•••••••

Special Events Tips: Always RSVP to an invitation in a timely fashion, even if you're not attending. For planned events, the host needs a definite head count by a specific date—this date is printed on the invitation. As a guest to a holiday party and/or other social gathering, your responsibilities begin when you receive an invitation. In the context of social invitations, RSVP is a process for a response from the invited person or people. It is derived from the French phrase Répondez s'il vous plaît meaning "Please respond" or literally, "Reply if you please." As a courtesy to the host, always reply (RSVP) to social invitations as soon as possible, immediately upon receipt is preferred, but definitely before the deadline. This will save the host/hostess time and money and will help the host to plan accordingly; space, activities, and food.

• • • • • • •

Kindness Fact: No act of kindness, no matter how small, is ever wasted.

●●●●●●●

KINDNESS: Today, put into practice a random act of kindness. Here are 20 ways you can sprinkle some joy. Kindness is contagious.

1. Send someone a handwritten note of thanks (just for being a friend).
2. Let someone ahead of you in the grocery store line, bank, post office, etc.
3. Make a card at home and send it to a friend for no reason.
4. Send someone in college a card of encouragement.
5. Buy a lottery ticket for a stranger.
6. Put some coins in someone else's parking meter.
7. Buy a coffee or a sandwich for the man selling newspapers on the street.
8. Give a compliment about your waiter/waitress to his/her manager.

9. Send someone a small gift anonymously.
10. Pay for the drinks on the next table at a café.
11. Treat a friend to the movies (just because).
12. Give a huge tip to someone when they least expect it.
13. Hold the door open for someone rushing to get in.
14. Give up your seat for someone, not just an elderly person.
15. Talk to a homeless person and have a "normal" conversation.
16. Pick up trash in the road, which would otherwise remain on the ground.
17. Compliment a work colleague for their excellence.
18. Give another driver your parking spot.
19. Call an elderly family member just to check on them.
20. Tell all your family members how much you appreciate them.

•••••••

Labor Day Etiquette Tip: On Labor Day you may wonder if white clothes should be retired until next year. In general, white is acceptable to wear after Labor Day and is not considered a fashion faux pas. Wear white any time of the year, especially if it looks good on you. However, when it comes to shoes, reserve all-white shoes (pumps, loafers, wedges, and sandals) for special occasions like weddings (most were designed for brides). An all-white boot is not practical for inclement weather and will draw a distracting amount of attention to your feet unless your entire outfit is white. I recommend wearing white with caution after Labor Day. Focus on variations of beige, cream and winter white. Wear outfits and colors that make you feel good, look great, and make you happy. Happy Labor Day!

"Never explain yourself to anyone. Because the person who likes you doesn't need it and the person who dislikes you won't believe it."

•••••••

Life/Business Etiquette Tip: Be mindful of what you say about others. Refrain from making offensive or degrading comments to or about another person's shortcomings. We all have shortcomings. Remember the old adage, "If you don't have something nice to say, then say nothing at all."

> People count up the faults of those who keep them waiting.
>
> French Proverb

•••••••

Life/Business Etiquette Tip: Don't interrupt: Interrupting someone who is speaking to add your own thoughts is impolite. Always wait until you're certain that the other person has finished before adding your own thoughts.

•••••••

Life/Business Etiquette Tip: In business and personal relationships, make every attempt to avoid these upcoming common mistakes, which could have a negative impact on your reputation and/or career.

• • • • • • •

Life/Business Etiquette Tip: Following up: Always follow up. Neglecting to follow this important tip shows that you are not proactive, uninterested in the company, and not serious about the opportunity.

• • • • • • •

May and June tend to be very busy months chock full of highly awaited graduations and other academic advancements. In particular, these momentous occasions are often accompanied by diligent searches for employment for some graduates. (See Interview Etiquette Tips)

• • • • • • •

Gentlemen: If a man is meeting a woman for a date, it will show he has manners if he arrives before his guest. Lateness of 5 to 10 minutes is acceptable, but should be prefaced with a phone call. Greater lateness (more than 10 minutes) should be explained as this can be very embarrassing to a lady.

• • • • • • •

Gentlemen: A man should open doors for a lady. What about car doors? A man should assist a lady into the car before letting himself into the car.

• • • • • • •

Gentlemen: Sending or hand delivering flowers to a lady is a thoughtful gesture for a special occasion or "just because" and never goes out of style. If a man is not sure what kind of flowers a lady likes or can't bring himself to ask her preference, then sending white flowers (carnations, chrysanthemums, or gardenias) or a single flower (rose) is acceptable.

• • • • • • •

Gentlemen: When a man accompanies a lady (whether on a date or not), the man should always assist her with her seat before taking his seat. The exception is booths.

• • • • • • •

Gentlemen: Today, hats are often worn by boys and men for style and/or practicality. Just a few decades ago, hats represented a code of respect and consideration, and gentlemen knew when it was acceptable to wear, remove, and when to tip their hats. Some hat rules have not changed. A man should remove his hat (hoods, etc.) upon entering a home, an office, a movie theatre, a restaurant, or a place of worship. He should remove his hat during the playing of the national anthem. He can keep his hat on in grocery stores, markets or other shops, in elevators, and in halls (of large buildings). Rule of thumb: When a man seats himself, he should take off his hat!

•••••••

New Year Etiquette Tip: New Year's Day wishes after the first seven days of the year should be avoided. If someone does offer you such a greeting after the first week into the New Year, don't be rude, thank them and move on. Wishing someone Happy New Year after the first week is like wishing someone Happy Valentine's Day on February 19.

•••••••

Nose Blowing Etiquette Tip: Nose blowing (at the table). Nose blowing at a table while dining should be avoided. It's common courtesy not to disgust or be off putting to others. Consider the fact that you may have to touch serving utensils or pass communal food dishes around the table. If you need to wipe your nose or if your nose begins to run after eating something spicy, then turn away from the table, subtly and gently wipe your nose with a tissue (not the cloth napkin). If you are caught off guard by an unexpected sneeze, use

> **Kindness is more important than perfection.**
>
> Unknown

your arm, not your hand to cover your nose. It's unreasonable to be expected to get up from the table and go to the restroom each and every time you have to sneeze, wipe or blow, especially if the restroom is some distance off. However, if you require a forceful, horn- honking nose blowing, or if you need to expel excessive mucus, or anything that could disgust others (picking or boring your nose), then this should be done in private. If you are ill and suffering from a runny nose or excessive sneezing, forego a dinner invitation, stay home and get well. Your thoughtfulness is greatly appreciated by all.

• • • • • • •

October is Breast Cancer Awareness Month, which is an annual campaign to increase awareness of the disease. (See Cancer Tips)

• • • • • • •

Office Etiquette Tip for Managers: Acknowledge when employees do a good job. If an employee is not doing a good job, speak with the employee in private. Never argue, discipline, or yell at an employee in front of other employees, customers, or management. Remember to praise in public and reprimand in private.

> Treat people as if they were what they ought to be and you help them to become what they are capable of being.
>
> Johann Wolfgang Von Goethe

• • • • • • •

Office Party Etiquette Tip: The holiday season brings office parties! Here are a few friendly reminders....so you will have no regrets on Monday.

• • • • • • •

Office Party Etiquette Tip: The holiday season is here and office parties have begun. Here are a few friendly reminders.

1. Stay for at least 30 minutes and make sure you network.
2. Don't stay until the doors close.
3. Don't drink too much alcohol. Overindulgence could cause you to do something that you may regret on Monday.
4. Attire—keep it simple. It may be a relaxed environment, but your attire should not be too relaxed, it should be professional.
5. Don't get too friendly with coworkers.
6. Remember to say thank you for being invited (food and drinks are extra costs for your employer), a simple thank you will show your appreciation to your employer and the party planning committee.

• • • • • • •

Opportunity: "Business opportunities are like buses, there's always another one coming." Richard Branson

•••••••

Pooch Etiquette: Dogs are social creatures and they love interacting with humans every day. Dog owners are encouraged to be mindful of pooch etiquette. Keep your dog leashed at all times (when out in public), especially on tracks, trails, and in bike/skate lanes. Some people aren't comfortable around dogs, but everyone has the right to enjoy the parks and trails.

•••••••

Pooch Etiquette: If your dog travels by car, be sure to secure your dog in a safe manner (lightweight carriers, doggy seatbelt, or car safety seat). Allow for frequent stops to let the dog exercise (keep him on a leash). If your dog travels by air, be sure to check with the airline about their rules well in advance. Each airline has slightly different requirements (some require the full airfare for pets).

> How can you squander even one more day not taking advantage of the greatest shifts of our generation? How dare you settle for less when the world has made it so easy for you to be remarkable?
>
> Seth Godin, Seth's Blog

● ● ● ● ● ● ●

Pooch Etiquette: Do not allow your dog in areas with posted signs such as children play areas, picnic areas, and athletic fields. Do not let your dog run up to anyone, bark loudly, chase anyone, or jump onto people to "say hello." Some people are not comfortable around dogs.

● ● ● ● ● ● ●

Pooch Etiquette: Pick up your dogs' waste immediately for disposal at your home or other designated receptacle. Check your local laws and codes. In some states, if you don't pick up after your dog, you could face a fine.

∙ ∙ ∙ ∙ ∙ ∙ ∙

Pooch Etiquette: Tie your dog to a chair and not a table when at a restaurant. Be sure that your dog does not sit in the waiter's path. Do not allow your dog to sit on chairs or tables. Do not allow your dog to drink out of the restaurant's glasses or dishes, unless they are disposable. It is appropriate to ask a waiter for a paper or plastic bowl for water, if necessary, but you should bring your own doggie bowl.

∙ ∙ ∙ ∙ ∙ ∙ ∙

Pooch Etiquette: Dog-friendly restaurants are gaining popularity. If you choose to dine out with your dog, first call and make sure an establishment allows dogs at their outdoor tables. Make sure your dog is well-behaved around other people, especially children.

∙ ∙ ∙ ∙ ∙ ∙ ∙

Pooch Etiquette: Some people have pet allergies, animal phobias, or may be nervous about pet accidents, etc. If your pet tends to have accidents when nervous or if your pet barks or howls constantly, please spare everyone else the drama and leave your darling pet at home.

• • • • • • •

Pooch etiquette during the Holidays: If you plan to take your pet along to holiday visits to see friends or relatives, don't assume that everyone is a pet person. Do not show up with an unannounced pet.

• • • • • • •

Pooch Etiquette: If you travel with your dog to a hotel that allows dogs, don't assume that everyone at the hotel is a dog person. Try to keep the barking to a minimum, walk your pet frequently, and please keep your dog on a leash.

•••••••

Pool Etiquette tip: Watch small children closely. Children are naturally drawn to water. You may have heard it before, but babies and small children can drown in just 1 inch of water. At pools and beaches, keep your eyes on babies and small children and stay within arms-reach at all times. Don't take your eyes off of them not even for one minute. Be safe and have fun!

•••••••

Pool Etiquette Tip: During your pool visit, if you borrow equipment that belongs to the pool site such as lawn chairs, water workout accessories, toys etc., then return borrowed items to their appropriate storage areas after use. Employ home principles: If you use something, replace it; If you borrow something, return it; If you mess up something, clean it up, etc.

•••••••

Pool Etiquette Tip: As temperatures heat up during summer months, pool and beach visits will increase. Friendly reminder: Do not distract the lifeguard. Do not ask the lifeguard to hold your belongings or to judge your swimming technique. Have fun, stay cool, and be safe.

•••••••

Pool Etiquette: Do not relieve yourself (pee) in the pool.

•••••••

Professional Etiquette Tip: Aim to keep your workspace and desk clean of food items. If most people in your office eat lunch around the same time, then distractions are usually minimal. However, if you eat lunch at your desk during odd hours or snacks throughout the day, be mindful of your coworkers. You should take care not to treat your workspace as a cafeteria or snack bar as the visual appearance of excessive food items, noise level of crunching and munching, and strong food odors emanating from the microwave (heavy spices, onions, and garlic) or bags of snack foods (potato chips, etc.) can be extremely annoying to your co-workers. Make sure that you discard trash and empty food and candy wrappers, smelly food containers, and empty soda cans, coffee cups, and water bottles. Wipe up any spills on your desk. Be mindful of the work environment. A smelly and messy workspace or desk can be distracting to co-workers and disruptive to the work flow.

> There's no substitute for good manners.
>
> Unknown

•••••••

Professional Etiquette Tip: Keep you your workspace clean. An unkempt and cluttered workspace is unattractive and distracting. According to a new survey of over 1,000 workers by staffing firm Adecco, a majority of Americans (57%) admit they judge coworkers by how clean or dirty they keep their workspaces. Meanwhile, nearly half say they have been "appalled" by how messy a colleagues' office is and most chalk it up to pure laziness. To read the full article, visit http://www.forbes.com/sites/jennagoudreau/2012/03/27/the-dangers-of-a-messy-desk/

• • • • • • •

Professional Etiquette Tip: Don't take your personal problems to work. I'm sure you have heard about many of your coworkers' problems, and you may have even shared a few of your problems while on the job. Coworkers and bosses will sometimes make decisions based on problems you may have shared. For example, if you confide in a "friend" or coworker that you were arrested over the weekend for driving under the influence after consuming one too many drinks during Happy Hour, you may later be required to take a random drug test or suffer other consequences at work.

• • • • • • •

Professional Etiquette Tip: Eliminate annoying habits (e.g., whistling, chewing, popping and/or cracking gum, speaking loudly, whispering, and clipping fingernails at the workstation). There are many others annoying habits. Which one grinds your gears?

"Politeness has become so rare that some people mistake it for flirtation."

• • • • • • •

Professional Etiquette Tip: Complete assignments on time and with minimal complaints. I challenged myself to go an entire day without complaining and thought it would be a piece of cake. Not! I discovered that my number one complaint was about other drivers/motorists, but of course, there were other complaints. Today's challenge—Go 24 hours without complaining about anything: spouse, children, parents, work, food, weather, traffic, etc. Report your results (just for fun).

> "Never borrow from the future. If you worry about it and it doesn't happen, you have worried in vain. If it does happen, you have to worry twice."

Professional Etiquette Tip: Arrive to work early rather than late.

Professional Etiquette Tip: Criticize in private. Praise in public.

Professional Etiquette Tip: If someone gets a promotion at work (even a rival), be gracious and congratulate him or her. Buy a congratulatory card, give a small gift, organize a celebration or invite him/her out to lunch.

Projects: "The successful always has a number of projects planned, to which he looks forward. Anyone of them could change the course of his life overnight." – Mark Caine

> Rudeness is the weak man's imitation of strength.
>
> Eric Hoffer

● ● ● ● ● ● ●

Respect Fact: Respect yourself and respect others. "Respect for ourselves guides our morals; respect for others guides our manners." – Laurence Sterne

● ● ● ● ● ● ●

RSVP is a French abbreviation (Répondez s'il vous plait) that simply means "Please reply" to the invitation with your intentions to attend (or decline). Your response will help the host or hostess to plan accordingly and prepare enough food for all guests.

> Failure seldom stops you. What stops you is the fear of failure.
>
> Jack Lemmon

•••••••

School Etiquette Tip: Teach children to love and respect teachers and administrators and never burn bridges. Being disrespectful is a quick way to burn a bridge. Solid and respectful relationships can open doors that may otherwise remain closed.

•••••••

School Etiquette Tip: Teach children to respect time. Do not show up too early and don't be late for school, appointments, meetings, etc. Explain the importance of meeting deadlines. Teach them to hand in deliverables on time: homework; assignments; papers; applications; exams; etc. Neglecting to meet deadlines can be very costly.

•••••••

School Etiquette Tip: Teach your child the importance of good sportsmanship; it's essential for getting along in this world. Sportsmanship applies on the court, on the field, and in the classroom. When someone gets a better grade or is recognized for an accomplishment (winning math bee), it's good form to say, "Congratulations!" When playing team games, remember that not everyone will be a winner (someone has to lose). Children should be taught how to lose gracefully.

> Seasons: One loss does not make a season.
>
> Unknown

• • • • • • •

School Etiquette Tip: Teach your child the importance of appearance and hygiene. Express how important it is to be clean and dress appropriately for school. This includes bathing, washing hands after using the restroom, eating, and brushing teeth. Avoid wearing clothing that is torn, dirty, or wrinkled.

•••••••

School Etiquette Tip: Teach children to follow the school rules about what is or is not allowed, including cell phones, medication, and other items.

•••••••

School Etiquette Tip: Remind children to be respectful of others, especially adults. Children should show respect to their teachers and use titles when speaking to adults; e.g., Miss., Mr., Mrs., and Ms.

•••••••

Self-care Etiquette Tip: It's great to give to others and organizations, but it's OK to start "giving" with you. Oftentimes we (especially women) deplete ourselves and our resources and have little time or anything left for ourselves. It's a blessing when you can give. But, please understand that it's not selfish to take care of oneself. Give yourself time to be still and gather your thoughts, give your body the water and nourishment it needs, give your body the physical exercise to improve every aspect of you, and give yourself permission to say NO to anything that does not work for you. TLF

•••••••

Social Etiquette Tip: Good manners can make you feel good. You can hold your head high when you are graceful and pleasant even under stressful circumstances.

•••••••

Social Etiquette Tip: Good manners build self-esteem. People (adults and teens) with high self-esteem are more likely to get what they want out of life.

•••••••

Social Etiquette Tip: Good manners are attractive.

•••••••

Social Media Etiquette Tip: Add a profile picture to all sites, especially sites used by business professionals (LinkedIn). Everyone likes to "see" who they are talking to and with whom they are doing business.

•••••••

Social Media Etiquette Tip: Don't post when you are angry, frustrated, or tired, and resist the urge to use profanity and foul language. Profanity directed at another can be offensive. If it is used to converse, it demonstrates a lack of social grace and can affect your credibility. Converse with intellect rather than profanity.

•••••••

Social Media Etiquette Tip: Consider every post. Your image is showing. Remember that everything you post is a reflection of you and your business. Don't post anything you don't want your customers/clients, employees, potential clients, or boss to see.

∙∙∙∙∙∙∙

Social Media Etiquette Tip: Don't make assumptions. Don't assume your friends or followers read every post. Friends and followers are inundated with posts. If you expect or desire feedback from a particular person on a particular post, reach out to them by other means.

∙∙∙∙∙∙∙

Social Media Etiquette Tip/Friendly Reminder: When someone posts something on Facebook and you wish to respond with a comment that is totally unrelated to the post, then start a new post, inbox the person, or send the person a private text message.

∙∙∙∙∙∙∙

Social Media Etiquette Tip: Be a good listener. For the people you follow or those with whom you do business or those with whom you like to engage, read their posts carefully and try to hear what is being said before chiming in. Hasty responses can sabotage personal and professional relationships.

• • • • • • •

Social Media Etiquette Tip: If you don't post anything for a long time, it's not necessary to apologize by sending a message, such as "Sorry I haven't posted anything lately." Just post something good.

• • • • • • •

Social Media is the way the vast majority of people communicate today (e.g., blogs, email, Facebook, Twitter, etc.). Etiquette tips will help you avoid faux pas when using these mediums.

•••••••

Social Media Etiquette: It is acceptable to NOT comment back on every single comment you receive.

•••••••

Social Media Etiquette: If you decide to unfriend/unfollow someone, just delete / leave. It is not necessary to make a big announcement.

•••••••

Social Media Etiquette Tip: Don't vent, rant, or speak negatively about coworkers, supervisors, or your job on social media sites. It's true that we have the freedom to do (and say) anything, but not everything is helpful. Your own words could cost you more than you imagine. If you need to vent, you may want to invest in and keep a journal to help you sort and collect your thoughts. Because after you hit send, electronic messages cannot be retrieved.

•••••••

Social Media Etiquette Tip: Don't allow social media to negatively affect your job performance by consuming your time that should be spent working, unless social media is your job and/or a function of your job or unless you are the boss. Otherwise, you could face unfortunate consequences from your employer if your activity is being monitored and if it can be proven that company time was abused and used for personal social media activity. Do not short change your employer. Give your employer the time that you are required to work and work every minute that you are being paid to work. If you find it difficult to resist the temptation to check your social accounts during work hours, then try leaving your electronic devices in your pocket, purse, car, locker, locked cabinet or other secure place until you have a break or lunch hour when you can freely check your accounts.

•••••••

Social Media Etiquette Tip: Don't be too quick to judge or react to every post you read. Take time to read and breathe before responding to posts from people who you may know, but may not know intimately. Knowing someone only via social media does not mean you know them intimately. Thus, false assumptions could be made about posts and/or relationships can suffer due to a presumably malicious post.

> It takes very little effort to be considered outstanding.
>
> Unknown

•••••••

Social Media Etiquette Tip: Social media has become a part of the fabric of our lives. It can be an asset or a liability. Don't let social media ruin relationships/friendships.

•••••••

Social Media Etiquette Tip: Do not spend time trying to guess a friend's motives for Facebook behaviors.

∙∙∙∙∙∙∙

Social Media Etiquette Tip: Don't take offense if everyone does not "like" every post.

∙∙∙∙∙∙∙

Social Media Etiquette Tip: Although people may like to support a business, cause, or event, they may not have the time or resources to donate. Take no offense (don't take it personal) if people do not choose to help.

∙∙∙∙∙∙∙

Social Media Etiquette Tip: Use the chat feature responsibly. Just because someone has a Facebook window open doesn't mean they're automatically available for a chat session (especially during business hours).

Social Media Etiquette Tip: Don't post anything that will hurt a friend's relationships.

• • • • • • •

> Don't wait for extraordinary opportunities. Seize common occasions and make them great.
>
> Orison Swett Marden

Social Media Etiquette Tip: Don't post anything that will hurt a friend's image or career.

• • • • • • •

Social Media Etiquette Tip: If you receive a friend request from a work colleague and choose not connect with them via Facebook, offer him/her an alternative. For example, "I do not connect with work contacts on Facebook, but please connect with me on LinkedIn."

• • • • • • •

Social Media Etiquette Tip: Do not post information on Facebook that could be used against you.

∙∙∙∙∙∙∙

Spa Etiquette Tip/Friendly Reminder: Remember to leave gratuity…..Gratuities are typically not included on services. If you were given a gift certificate, ask if the tip was included. The proper tip is 15% to 20%. Gratuity is optional, but always appreciated.

∙∙∙∙∙∙∙

Spa Etiquette Tip: What to wear… Wear clothing that is comfortable and clean and makes you feel relaxed. Some people choose to wear bathing suits or under garments. Whatever you choose, remember that the therapists are trained to keep you properly and modestly dressed during your treatments, and are highly trained to respect your privacy.

∙∙∙∙∙∙∙

Spa Etiquette Tip: Check the spa cancellation policy when you make your reservation. Do this to avoid unnecessary charges (cancellation fees). Life happens when we have other plans.

•••••••

Spa Etiquette Tip: Arrive a little early. Always arrive at least 20 minutes early. This will allow you time to relax and de-stress before your scheduled reservation, change your clothes and prepare for your service. Turn-off or mute your electronic devices (tablets, cell phones, iPods, etc.) as a courtesy to other spa patrons and in honor of the peaceful spa environment. Relax and enjoy!

•••••••

Day Spa/Salon Etiquette Tip: Check the spa child policies before your visit. There are many child friendly salons and numerous Day Spas for Kids. However, in general, salons and kids don't mix. The salon is a place to relax and enjoy many salon services (massages, facials, hairdos, etc.). For many adults, it is the only time or place they can go when they are not accompanied by their children and a place where they expect to enjoy themselves without distractions from other children. Thus, make every effort to enjoy the spa without your children in tow. Firstly, babies and small children should not be expected to sit quietly and not make any noise for extended periods. Secondly, babies and children need supervision at all times, therefore, if you cannot properly supervise children during your spa service, then they should be under another's care. Thirdly, if you had arranged for childcare and your arrangements fell through, then postponing /rescheduling or cancelling should be considered. Consider others and check salon child policy before your visit (whether you plan to take a child/children with you or would rather not visit a salon that is child friendly).

• • • • • • •

Spa Etiquette Tip: Do not take babies and small children to your spa appointment. Babies and small children require constant attention. Your spa treatment/service is a time for you to relax and de-stress. As a courtesy to other spa patrons and in honor of the peaceful spa environment, avoid taking children with you to the spa!

●●●●●●●

Success: "Most successful men have not achieved their distinction by having some new talent or opportunity presented to them. They have developed the opportunity that was at hand." – Bruce Barton

●●●●●●●

Success: "Wherever you see a successful business, someone once made a courageous decision." – Peter Drucker

●●●●●●●

Successful Parenting: If your children feel safe, wanted, and loved, you are a successful parent.

•••••••

Summer picnic etiquette tip: Don't overdo it. When serving yourself, don't pile your plate. You can always go back for seconds. Piling your plate makes it look like you only showed up for the food.

•••••••

Summer Picnic Etiquette Tip: Keep an eye on your children. Don't get so caught up in the festivities (talking, texting, looking at photos, surfing the internet, dancing, etc.) that you lose sight of your children. Children move quickly and get into things oftentimes before anyone notices. Stay alert and pay attention to your children at all times.

•••••••

Summer is in full swing and travel is on the rise. With our busy lives, we can sometimes discover that we have forgotten an item that we need, after we arrive at our destination. Here is a checklist to make summer travel packing a breeze. A printable copy is available at www.theetiquetteconsultinggroup.com

•••••••

SUMMER TRAVEL CHECKLIST

Personal Hygiene
- Eye glasses, contacts & solution, eye drops
- Medication/vitamins
- Hair products (shampoo, conditioner, etc.)
- Hair grooming items (comb/brush)
- Curling irons, flat irons, straitening devices
- Sunscreen
- Soap/Lotion
- Tooth brush/Toothpaste
- Deodorant
- Razors and shaving cream
- Cologne/perfume

Clothing
- Undergarments
- Day wear
- Evening wear
- Swim wear
- Workout gear
- Foot wear
- Head wear (sun visors, head bands, hats)

Accessories
- Jewelry (Cuff links)
- Scarves/wraps/jackets

Electronics
- Cell phone
- IPod/computer/tablet
- Chargers
- Camera
- Ear bubs – head phones

Money & Documents
- Driver's license
- Registration

- Cash/credit cards/debit cards, traveler's checks
- Passport
- Printouts (flight/rental car/hotel/travel itinerary/driving directions)
- Boarding pass

Additional Items
- Books/journals/magazines
- Snacks
- Hand sanitizer/ Disposable wipes
- Eye mask
- Ear plugs

• • • • • • •

Summer Event Invitation Etiquette: Summer is filled with celebrations of all sorts: weddings, receptions, bridal / baby showers, graduation parties, and other events. We may find ourselves on all three sides of a guest list–inviter, invited, and uninvited. If we haven't been invited intentionally (possibly for factors that we aren't even aware of), lack of space, a different crowd, or as a plain oversight, we should make every effort not to take it personally. There is no socially acceptable way to bring up a party that we weren't invited to. It will be awkward and uncomfortable. The best thing to do is to leave it alone. While you may be hurt, angry, upset, offended or disappointed, you should not feel bad about yourself. Don't start questioning yourself, examining your flaws, or stewing over possible reasons. The reason you weren't invited may have absolutely nothing to do with you. Be gracious and polite regardless of another person's decision. You can say to the host something like, "I know you probably couldn't invite everyone, and I totally understand. I'm sure it was/will be a lovely affair and I wish you or the honoree(s) well."

• • • • • • •

Summer Travel Tip: Pack one change of clothes in your carry-on bag. Each year approximately 30 million pieces of luggage are lost, misplaced, or delayed. If this happens to you, at least you will have one set of clothes to change into, while you wait for your lost luggage.

•••••••

Summer Picnic Etiquette Tip: Don't be the guest who won't leave. When the host starts gathering used glasses and dirty dishes, starts putting away food, and infers that the party is over, take these queues, thank the host, and make an exit (unless you're helping with the cleanup).

•••••••

Summer Picnic/Party Etiquette Tip: Summer is the time for picnics and barbeques (a.k.a. cookouts) Don't take uninvited guests to your friends' home, barbeque, or party without giving the host advance notice. Giving advance notice is common courtesy and helps to avoid awkward situations.

•••••••

Photo Tag Etiquette: Be mindful of who you tag in photos. And be sensitive of the photos you share

> **Success is the sum of small efforts, repeated day in and day out.**
>
> **Robert Collier**

of yourself and others, whether they are family, friends, or coworkers. Posting inappropriate or very personal photos may seem harmless to someone, but could be awkward for another or cost another person his or her job or relationship.

•••••••

Photo Untagging Etiquette: It is acceptable to untag yourself from any photograph. The only caveat is that untagging is permanent: You can't be retagged to a photo once the tag is removed.

•••••••

Text Message Etiquette Tip and Friendly Reminder. Text responsibly. Don't text while walking.

Text Message Etiquette Tip: When responding to group text messages, avoid responding to the entire group. Respond to the sender only. This will avoid confusion.

Text Message Etiquette: Read, re-read, and read again before you send a text. Once it's sent, it's visible. Don't rely on recall features (Microsoft Outlook and other software) because these features have limitations.

Time: Cherish this day and every moment that you have with loved ones and friends!!!

Tipping Etiquette Tips (no pun intended)
Summer Travel: If you are traveling during the summer, then be sure to factor tipping into your plans. Leaving gratuity is optional, but can make a big difference in the life of those who work hard, but earn little or receive little recognition.

AIRPORTS

- Curbside check-in – $1.00 per bag. If you have three bags, tip $5.00. More bags, tip up proportionally. Feel free to tip up for this service.

- Shuttle driver from the terminal to the rental car agency or offsite parking: $1.00 per person, more if the driver helped load your bags.

- Taxi: 15% of the fare, more if the driver is helpful with bags. Tip at least $1.00, even for short rides.

TOUR GUIDES

- Tour Guide – Touring the city? Make sure to

thank your guide. Average $3.00 to $5.00 per person (adults – no need to include babies and toddlers)

RESTAURANTS & CARRY-OUTS

- Waiters & waitresses: 15% to 20% at buffet (10%)
- Maître d (m⁻a-tr-d⁻e – head waiter) – special reservations slip $10 or $20
- Outback Steakhouse carryout if someone brings food to your car: 10%
- Delivery to your home/hotel room: 10% – 20%
- If you sit at the bar, tip bartender $1 to $2 per drink. If you are there several hours, tip 10% – 20% of your bill.

HOTELS

- Valet – No need to tip when you arrive. However, when the car is returned to you, tip $2 -$5

- Doorman – No tip required for opening the door. Tip $1.00 for hailing you a cab, more if he did so in inclement weather.

- Bellman – $1.00 per bag plus extra if he provides you with information about your hotel or the local area.

- Concierge – No tip is required for general hotel information like, "What time is breakfast?" You do tip for any special service such as booking tours, making outside reservations, providing printed directions, reserving a car, etc. How much to tip depends: $2.00 for printed directions up to $20 or more for making special arrangements.

•••••••

Hotel Dining Room: Same as restaurant tipping (see above).

- In-room dining: A service charge will be added to your bill, but that goes to the hotel, not usually to the person delivering your meal. Add at least 10%, not less than $3.00.

- Maid: This is the most overlooked tip! When staying for more than one night, tip at least $1.00 per day, per person. Place the tip each morning on the desk with a note that says, "For our Maid" so she knows it's hers. You can also write a short thank-you. Something like, "Good morning! Thank you for everything, our room looks great!"

•••••••

Valentine's Day Tip: Enjoy this day no matter what! Count your blessings. Take some time to tell someone how much you love and appreciate them; your significant other, parent(s), child/children, sibling, loved one, or a friend. Somebody needs an extra dose of love today. Show your love!

•••••••

Wardrobe/Appearance Etiquette Tip: Dress appropriately for your profession to increase your credibility. Your image is showing and your appearance is your "Visual résumé." Most people want to be perceived as professional and competent by their clients or colleagues. Does your "visual résumé" contribute to that perception or weaken it?

• • • • • • •

Wedding Etiquette Tip: Firm but gentle advice to wedding guests. Please respect our privacy. No social media postings please!!! Our photographer will capture how this moment looks. We encourage you all to capture how it feels with your hearts, without the distraction of technology.

• • • • • • •

Winter Weather Tip: During winter months, keep a shovel and/or salt in your car if you plan to drive where there may be snow and/or ice. If you encounter an impasse, you will be prepared. Other items to keep with you: blanket, bottled water, non-perishable food items (protein bars), flash light, cell phone, and batteries.

∙∙∙∙∙∙∙

Workplace Etiquette Tip For Managers: Be approachable and have an open door policy as you train and mentor employees.

∙∙∙∙∙∙∙

Workplace Etiquette Tip For Managers: Be responsible and respect other people's time when scheduling meetings. Start and end on time.

∙∙∙∙∙∙∙

Workplace Etiquette Tip For Managers: Always communicate (verbal and written communication) in a professional and polite manner to employees and management.

> Treat everyone with politeness, even those who are rude to you — not because they are nice, but because you are.
>
> Unknown

Workplace Etiquette Tip: Similar to a disheveled appearance foul language can impact the way you're perceived by others in the workplace. Refrain from swearing, cussing, or cursing at work. Others are watching (coworkers, clients, customers, and bosses). Swearing when you hit your knee against your desk or when books get dropped on your toes or your computer crashes is one thing, swearing like a sailor on a daily basis is another. Using bad language can call your professionalism into question. Furthermore, it can be viewed as lack of self-control, immaturity or make it seem as if your vocabulary is limited. Words have the power to crush, cut, offend, and so much more. Exercise self-control and choose your words wisely. Choose words that soothe and heal.

•••••••

Yoga/Bikram Yoga Etiquette Tip: Do not bring cell phones in the hot room. Lockers are provided for your belongings and doors are kept locked during class. Some people think that bringing a cell phone and setting it on vibrate is being considerate. However, vibrating phones can be just as annoying in spa-like environments where stillness and silence are strongly desired. As a courtesy to other yogis and in honor of the peaceful environment, do not bring cell phone in the hot room.

•••••••

Yoga/Bikram Yoga Etiquette Reminder: Yoga/Bikram Yoga is a wonderful stress reliever. But, when people ignore codes of conduct, tensions can rise. The hot room should be quiet both before and after each class. This is a space that many people use to re-center and relax. Please respect your neighbors and keep your conversations isolated to the areas outside of the hot room.

Dear Reader,

If you have other topics and/or etiquette tips and would like to share, write them down along with your name, address, and tip/topic and email or mail to me. I welcome the opportunity to share with other readers in a future book. Many thanks!

Tamlyn L. Franklin
808 Gleneageles Ct #42141
Towson, MD 21286

Email: Tamlyn.Franklin@theecgi.com